The Dreidel's Hidden Meanings

The Mysteries of Judaism Series

The Dreidel's
Hidden Meanings

Rabbi Yitzchak Ginsburgh

Gal Einai

Jerusalem • New York • Los Angeles

The Mysteries of Judaism Series
The Dreidel's Hidden Meanings

Rabbi Yitzchak Ginsburgh

Printed in the United States of America

Ordering Information:

Gal Einai Institute
1651 President St.
2nd Floor
Brooklyn, NY 11213
webstore: www.innermedia.org

For information:

email: innerstudy@gmail.org
internet: www.inner.org

GAL EINAI produces and publishes books, pamphlets, and recorded lectures by Rabbi Yitzchak Ginsburgh. All of our products can be purchased online at www.innermedia.org.

ISBN: 978-965-7146-38-5

Chanukah and the Dreidel

Uniting the Supernatural and Natural

We light Chanukah candles to publicize the miraculous power of God who intervened on behalf of the Maccabees. The eight days of Chanukah commemorate the miraculous lighting of the seven-branched Menorah in the Holy Temple for eight days, thus connecting the numbers 7 and 8 together. In Jewish tradition, the number 7 represents a state of natural perfection (for example, Shabbat, is the seventh day of the week), but the number 8 represents a state of supernatural perfection (for example, circumcision is done on the child's eighth day). Thus, Chanukah unites the natural with the supernatural, the finite with the infinite.

The Ba'al Shem Tov, the founder of the Chassidic movement, possessed a special love and affinity for Chanukah more than all the other holidays of the year. This is because the Chanukah candles represent the innate gift of the Jewish soul for spreading light and illuminating the whole world (even the non-Jewish world). The Ba'al Shem Tov's message spread by the Jewish soul stresses both that God creates nature anew at every moment and at the same time permeates it with supernatural power. Because of its ability to unite the natural with the supernatural, the light of the Chanukah candles will eventually bring about the true and complete redemption.

The Dreidel

A very popular Jewish custom is to play dreidel on Chanukah. Adults together with children gather around the lights of the *menorah*, spinning to discover which letter falls on top. What is the deeper significance of this act, and what meaningful thoughts can we have in mind while playing dreidel this Chanukah? As we will see, by spinning the dreidel in front of the Chanukah lights, we are bridging the gap between the finite realm and the infinite.

The Dreidel's Four Letters

By tradition, the dreidel has four faces. The first thing one notices about the dreidel is that each of the dreidel's four faces has one of the letters of the Hebrew alphabet inscribed on it. The four letters are *nun* (נ), *gimel* (ג), *hei* (ה), and *shin* (ש), the initials of the phrase, "A great miracle occurred there" (נֵס גָּדוֹל הָיָה שָׁם).

The first thing to note is that the numerical value of these four letters together, נגהש, is 358, also the numerical value of Mashiach (מָשִׁיחַ)! The recurring motif found in the dreidel's hidden meanings is that of the Mashiach and redemption—changing the world and making it a worthy dwelling place for the Almighty.

In the past generation, some Jews living in the Land of Israel decided that it would be proper to change the last word from "there" (שָׁם) to "here" (פֹּה) thus making the phrase whose initials are on the dreidel, "A great miracle occurred here."

Following this idea, the letters on the dreidel would be *nun*, *gimel*, *hei*, and *pei*, נגהפ, and their numerical sum would come to 138. But, as it is, you cannot escape the dreidel's inner meaning, and 138 is the value of Menachem (מְנַחֵם), one of the names of the Mashiach according to the sages; it is also the value of the word *Tzemach* (צֶמַח), the name of the Mashiach appearing in the Bible, "Tzemach is his name...."[1]

When a Square Becomes a Circle

The dreidel is shaped like a top, with a pointed bottom edge on which it can be spun. Spinning the dreidel causes its square contours to fade-out, making it seem like a round top.

Conceptually, the dreidel's square faces and features represent the mathematical and syllogistic logic of the ancient Greeks, over whom the Maccabee's were victorious, both materially and spiritually. The Maccabee's, true to our faith in one God, believed and indeed practiced their belief that a view of nature and life that is based on human rationalism alone is lacking, for it is the infinite God, who has no bounds that brings all of reality into being. Thus, the round contours revealed by the dreidel when it spins represent the realm of the Divine, which manifests as miracles[2]—events that cannot be understood, and sometimes even perceived—by the rational human mind.

To call upon the terminology of Chassidut, the round contours of the spinning dreidel represent the revelation of God's surrounding light,[3] referring to the energy with which the Almighty sustains reality. This aspect of God is described as round because He sustains all of reality equally, from the minutest particle to the greatest super cluster of galaxies. Just as the circle has no top and bottom and all its points are equivalent, so from the perspective of God's surrounding light, all of reality is equally important and therefore continually sustained. Just as God sustains the laws of nature at every moment, so He is privy to altering them.

The dreidel's square shape represents the ever-present experience of God's inner light,[4] referring to the energy with which the Almighty is perceived by our consciousness. The capacity to reveal Divinity changes from one part of nature to another just as the ability to perceive God varies from one individual to the other. For this reason, God's inner light is likened to a straight line (the contours of the dreidel's faces are straight lines), which has both a beginning and an end, indicating gradation.[5]

The surrounding (round) light reveals God's infinite nature; the inner light (square) reveals His finite nature. It is from God's surrounding light—from His infinite nature—that miracles happen.

Thus, we are not the only ones playing dreidel. In a sense, whenever a miracle occurs, we can imagine that God too has been playing with His big cosmic dreidel. By spinning this abstract dreidel, God spins His inner light—His revealed finite nature as we experience it normally—blurring the harsh logical rules that govern reality and allowing His infinite nature to be revealed. One might say that God is continually spinning miracles into nature.

By meditating on the act of spinning our own physical dreidel, we connect and identify with the Divine and show our willingness to see beyond the square and logical face of nature and believe and tap into the infinite, circular realm of God's infinite space. In effect, meditating on the dreidel's spin has the power to open our eyes to miracles.

What's in a Name?

To gain a deeper appreciation of this charming little toy, let us continue by analyzing its name. As is well known, the name of an object (particularly in Hebrew) reveals its essence. The dreidel has three names that we are going to look at it. First, in Hebrew it is called a *sevivon* (סְבִיבוֹן); obviously, this is the most sacred name of the three. In Yiddish, it is called a dreidel, the name that it is most commonly known by around the Jewish world. Finally, in English, we would call it a "top."

Hebrew: Sevivon

In Hebrew, the dreidel is called a *sevivon* (סְבִיבוֹן). The root of this word means "to spin." Since we have already spent some time addressing the dreidel's spin, let us begin our analysis of its Hebrew name from a numerical perspective.

The numerical value of *sevivon* (סְבִיבוֹן) is 130, which is also the numerical value of the Hebrew word for "eye" (עַיִן).[6] The *sevivon* represents the eye that sees the Divine spinning within the natural world. The person with *sevivon*-vision sees reality as it truly is, allowing him to experience the ever-spinning Divine consciousness into his life, while staying focused and precise.

This connection between the dreidel, eyesight, and Chanukah is best illustrated by the *mitzvah* of Chanukah itself: lighting candles. Though we are required to gaze at the candles of the *menorah*, we are prohibited from using them for any purpose whatsoever. Our obligation is simply to look at the light emitted by the candles, letting it shine Divine revelation into the depth of our souls. The power of the Chanukah candles is spiritual, which is why they cannot and should not be used materially. Light from the Chanukah candles has the power to vanquish all negative forces, cultures, and beliefs. Gazing at it emblazes our own consciousness with the ability to truly see reality for what it is—an expression of the Divine.

After gazing at the light of the candles and recalibrating our vision, we can exercise our renewed spiritual vision by spinning the dreidel, the *sevivon*, whose *gematria* alludes to the inner eye that we have awakened. Through play, we begin to let our newly rectified vision of reality express itself. Seeing the finite and separate myriad particulars of the world (as represented by the dreidel's square shape) wholly subsumed within Divine consciousness (the dreidel's spin).

The Sevivon and the Secret of the Eye

In Hebrew, the eyeball is referred to as the "wheel of the eye"[7] (גַּלְגַּל הָעַיִן). Perhaps the greatest secret of the eye's anatomy and functionality is that for the information it passes to the brain to be interpretable as an image of our surroundings, the eye must continually be moving. Like a wheel that is continually turning, the eye rotates fractionally (with very minute movements, to and fro), observing reality and picking up light from our surroundings.

What is true for physical vision is even more so for spiritual vision—our ability to see how Divinity is vested in everything. Normally, we do not sense Divinity and imagine that God is transcendent but not immanent. In Chassidut, seeing beyond the Godless physical appearance of reality is termed seeing past the initial contraction of God's infinite light. Honing our ability to see spiritually also improves our ability to see physically. When all details of reality are perceived as existing within the infinite light of God, the eye perceives with greater precision and clarity.

Seeing Variety

Even once we have begun to perceive God manifest in reality, our first approximation is usually to imagine that all is (or at least should be) the same, preventing us from finding value in variety.[8] When first becoming aware of the Divine enclothed within the mundane, an individual is blinded, so to speak, and can therefore really only make out a single brilliant light. It turns out that the dreidel is the perfect object of meditation with which to lift this limitation.

The ability of an ordinary eye is limited so that whenever anything rotates very quickly or rapidly, we lose our ability to pick up details. By contrast, the power of the Jewish eye is to capture the four faces phased out by the *sevivon's* spin. To use the *sevivon* to better our eyesight translates into being able to distinguish between its four faces even when it is spinning. To truly perfect our spiritual and physical eyesight we can imagine seeing each face clearly even while the dreidel approaches an infinite rotational velocity.

Let us use another metaphor to make this point more clearly. We are probably all familiar with a color wheel, a circle on which the basic colors appear like the slices of a pie. When the wheel is turned rapidly the individual colors blend into one another, disappear, and it seems the entire wheel is colored white; the velocity of the rotation makes everything appear homogeneous. Essentially, even though God is one, i.e., homogeneous, the infinite variety that we find in mundane reality (even in holiness) has its source in the Creator.

Having a spiritual eye can be likened to being able to focus on a spinning color wheel yet still being able to clearly pick out individual colors. Likewise, the Jewish (spiritual) eye, trained and refined by the study of Kabbalah and Chassidut, allows us to zone into reality, picking up the (normally submerged) individual hues of Divinity within each of its parts. By studying the inner teachings of the Torah, the eye becomes rectified enough to see the Divine source of every detail. Indeed, the Creator has both a finite and an infinite nature and the finite continues to exist within God's infinite nature.[9] Given an eye for spiritual details, one can see how every aspect of the mundane can be found in the Divine with wonderful clarity.

The same effect can be found in the spinning dreidel. The dreidel's speed makes its distinct faces blur together. But, a person with this *sevivon*-vision will see be able to perceive each of the four faces and the letters inscribed on them with perfect clarity. Otherwise, we have to wait for the dreidel to slow down, tip over, and fall down.

An Eye for Mashiach

Perhaps the most meaningful secret of spinning the dreidel is that a person with *sevivon*-vision also has the ability to open his eyes to see the Mashiach. As noted, the numerical value of the letters inscribed on the dreidel's four faces amount to 358, the same as Mashiach.

The Lubavitcher Rebbe impressed upon us many times that the Mashiach is already present in our midst and that the only thing we need to do is open our eyes to see him. Thus, spinning the dreidel and developing our spiritual eyesight is perhaps the best possible exercise for opening our eyes and perceiving the presence of the Mashiach.

Yiddish: Dreidel

The word dreidel in Yiddish, like its Hebrew counterpart, stems from the verb meaning to spin. When transliterated into Hebrew,[10] the Yiddish word "dreidel" (דְרֵידְל) equals 248. The prophets[11] stated that the Mashiach will arrive, riding on a donkey. Interestingly, the value of "donkey" (חֲמוֹר) is also 248, the same *gematria* as dreidel. Connecting this with our observation that the value of the letters on the dreidel equals the value of Mashiach, we can surmise that metaphorically speaking, Mashiach will come riding on (i.e., as a result of) the opening of our eyes to see the Divine root of all mundane reality by spinning the dreidel.

Dreidel—248—is also the *gematria* of Abraham (אַבְרָהָם). The first dreidel then is the figure of Abraham himself, a person who revolved around the world in order to reveal God's presence and universal goodness to all of mankind. In this sense, every Jewish soul descended from Abraham is a dreidel. Abraham traveled to and fro through the world in an attempt to free the holy sparks of Divinity.

The Hebrew word for "merchant" (סוֹחֵר) stems from the same root as the root meaning "to circle"; a merchant, like the dreidel, is constantly circling in search of profit. Abraham too was a merchant and his wares were consciousness of God. This is also the hidden reason that many Jews throughout the generations have made their living as merchants. A Jew is always looking for an opportunity to make a profit. Of course, real and lasting profit involves spreading Divine consciousness. Today, many of us spend almost as much time spinning in the air on airplanes as traveling on land, but it is a basic property of the Jewish soul we are always running to and fro through the world.

The Chassidic dreidel-figure is the Ba'al Shem Tov who spun around and around the world in order to teach the miraculous, to help spread the awareness of God and the supernatural. The Ba'al Shem Tov was a miracle worker, a *tzadik* for whom Chanukah had a constant inner presence in his soul. The Chanukah lights, a product of the faith of Israel, have the power to overcome heresy and the Hellenism of cultures that do not believe in what the physical eye cannot directly observe. The Ba'al Shem Tov spun his way past disbelief in an effort to help the simple folk of his time serve God. He showed these goodhearted Jews how finitude truly exists in a state of infinitude. Or, to use the metaphor from the dreidel, how the dreidel's four faces are forever present no matter how fast it is spinning. In short, he taught them how to see reality with *sevivon*-vision.

English: Top

The English word that best describes the dreidel is a "top." Transliterating this word into Hebrew yields the word meaning "an infant," or "child" (טַף). Indeed, sometimes transliteration reveals surprising connections between words in Hebrew, the holy language with which God spoke the world into being, and other languages. The transliterated form of "top" is also a two-letter root which expands into the root meaning "to take care of" (טָפַל),[12] another link with the top being a children's toy.[13]

Most amazingly, the numerical value of the transliterated form of "top" (טָף) is 89, which is also the numerical value of Chanukah (חֲנוּכָּה)—signifying that the best time to play with a top is indeed on Chanukah (with children, of course)!

Top, Tip, Fall

We can continue to expand our meditation on the transliterated form of top by noting that the dreidel passes through three stages each time it is spun.

First, by spinning it, it enters a more or less steady state of rotation in which it is standing upright (hence the name, "top"). As it loses speed, the dreidel begins to wobble and tip over. Finally, the dreidel falls over completely and stops. We can characterize these three stages with the words, top, tip, and fall.

If we use the transliterated form of "top" (טָף) then the Hebrew words describing these three stages are all found to be transliterations of the English words, indicating a very strong relationship between the concepts in Hebrew and English. Something that is tipping over, as is the dreidel in the second stage, is in need of care (טִיפּוּל), whose first three letters are the transliterated form of "tip" (טִיפ). Finally, falling over is most explicitly an English word which comes from Hebrew (נוֹפֵל).

The Miracle in Falling

All this may seem to shed little light on the dreidel until we note that the word for "falling over" (נוֹפֵל) is in Hebrew also grammatically related to the word for "wonder" (פֶּלֶא). This suggests that even though we normally associate falling with something negative, the dreidel's spin and fall (with the fall revealing a particular letter) reveals that there is actually something wondrous about falling.

We might expect that the letter on which the dreidel has landed be the one at the bottom, the one inscribed on the face touching the floor. But, as the game is traditionally played, the dreidel is considered to have landed on the letter facing up. In other words, even though this letter is the one on which the dreidel has fallen it has been elevated and lifted to face upwards.

This reversal of fortune, as we might describe it, is truly wondrous. It suggests that that which a moment ago was falling face down has suddenly flipped upside-down and been taken to a higher place. This reversal represents the letter being returned to its infinite source in God (who is symbolically associated with being above,[14] even though God is of course everywhere). We can think of the dreidel as a centrifuge, which after spinning at high speeds separates out something (a letter) that is both surprising (1 out of 4 possibilities) and miraculous (because it has been elevated from the lowest place).[15]

Following our current analysis, the first two stages (the dreidel spinning and then tipping over, about to fall) represent states of instability. But, once the dreidel has actually fallen over and one letter has singled out and returned to its spiritual source above, the dreidel has reached a rectified state of stability. It is very appropriate then that there should be instilled from a young age, excitement as to which letter lands on top. It is as if the dreidel prompts us to wait for that which has fallen to return back to God.

Spinning around until one falls in a certain place is something that Jews are very familiar with. Clearly, describing the dreidel's motion in this manner parallels the states of exile and redemption. The first two stages (spinning and tipping over) are states of exile, which pertains to individuals as much as to the entire Jewish nation. When starting out in adulthood, one usually experiences a period that can be described as spinning around, looking for one's place and role in the world. Sometimes this period may last for many years. But, eventually, one falls in a certain place. The message is that wherever one has fallen down, there is something to elevate their; there is a particular aspect of Divinity that one has been given the task of redeeming and elevating in that space. Thus, the third stage—falling and facing upwards—represents a state of redemption, in which the redeemed return to their origin.

Here again, the spinning dreidel reminds us of the merchant's wandering to and fro, like the Jew who while exiled from the Land of Israel travels through the world searching for spark of holiness (both physical and intellectual) to redeem. The dreidel tipping over suggests that we are all in need of support and care from above, care that represents God's intervention by beginning to redeem us from our exile. Finally, the last stage represents our wondrous and surprising return to God.[16] Let us summarize the three stages of the dreidel's movement in a chart:

dreidel's state	English & transliteration	meaning	symbolic of
spinning	top (סֵף)	child	Jewish people in exile
slowing down and tipping over	tip (טִיפּוּל)	a person or object in need of being taken care of	beginning of rectification process
letter lands on top	fall (נוֹפֵל)	fall and wonder at the Divine Providence revealed	Jewish people returns to their Source

The Dreidel's Four Faces

The Essence of the Four Faces

Whenever we have a structure made up of 4 elements it is essential to Jewish meditation to establish a correspondence between the 4 elements and the 4 letters of God's essential Name, *Havayah* (יהוה). Since the dreidel has 4 faces, our understanding of its symbolism will not be complete without drawing such a correspondence.

We have two models before us: the 4 faces of the dreidel and the four letters of *Havayah*. Creating correct parallels between models is the foundation of all mystical thought as it allows us to extend our understanding. The model of God's essential Name, *Havayah* has been discussed extensively elsewhere, so we will immediately proceed to how each letter corresponds to one of the dreidel's faces.

The basis for drawing this correspondence lies in first establishing to which of the four directions (north, south, east, and west) each of the four letters inscribed on the dreidel corresponds. It is well-known how the four directions correspond to the four letters of *Havayah*.

- נ – The *nun* if the first letter of the word "miracle," which in Hebrew also means a "banner," or "flag" suggesting that miracles are something that should be publicly displayed and taken note of. The banner that God waves every morning—broadcasting to the world that all of a nature is actually miraculous—is the rising of the sun in the east. Indeed, the verse describing the essence of the letter *nun* (נ)—the initial letter of "miracle" and the letter inscribed on the dreidel—is "Before the sun, his name is Yinon"[17] (לִפְנֵי שֶׁמֶשׁ יִנּוֹן שְׁמוֹ). This verse explicitly connects the letter *nun* (*Yinon*, another name ascribed to the Mashiach) with the sun. So the letter *nun* corresponds with the east.

- ג – The *gimel* is the first letter of the word "great" (גָּדוֹל), suggesting the *sefirah* of loving-kindness and the character of Abraham (the archetypal soul of loving-kindness) who is described as "the great man among giants"[18] (הָאָדָם הַגָּדוֹל בָּעֲנָקִים). From the moment Abraham received the command to "Go for yourself… to the land that I will show you,"[19] all his travels were towards the south (of the Land of Israel).[20] Thus, we associate the *gimel* with the south.

- ה – The *hei* is the initial letter of the word "occurred" (הָיָה). The miracle the idiom inscribed on the dreidel refers to is the miracle of one cruse of oil lighting the Temple Menorah for eight days (when normally the quantity is only enough for one day). The Menorah, which in the Temple had 7 candles, was made of pure gold. There is a great deal of discussion in Chassidut regarding the manner in which gold defined the function of the Menorah as the spiritual source of (understanding and) sustenance for all seven categories of Jewish souls.[21] In fact, the letters of the Hebrew word for "gold" (זָהָב) can be interpreted as an equation describing the Temple Menorah's structure: 7 (ז) = 5 (ה) ⊥ 2 (ב). The Menorah's 7 candles were divided into 5 and 2.[22] The verse explicitly states that "From the north comes gold…"[23] (מִצָּפוֹן זָהָב יֶאֱתֶה), and so the *hei* of the dreidel is clearly identified with the north, which in Kabbalah is the direction of the *sefirah* of understanding.

- שׁ – The letter *shin* is the first letter of the word "there" (שָׁם). In general, the word "there" is associated with the west, the direction representing the Divine Presence (the innermost chamber of the Temple, the Holy of Holies, was to the west). The Divine Presence is also referred to as the Name (שֵׁם), as in the words said immediately after the first verse of the *Shema*, "Blessed be the Name of the glory of His kingdom for ever and ever."[24]

Let us summarize our correspondence so far in a chart,

face of dreidel	direction
gimel (ג)	south
hei (ה)	north
nun (נ)	east
shin (שׁ)	west

The next step then is to use this correspondence to complete our parallel. The south is associated with the *sefirah* of wisdom, as the sages say, "One who wants to be wise should travel to the south."[25] Since the *sefirah* of wisdom corresponds to the *yud* of *Havayah*, we have found that the dreidel's *gimel* corresponds to the *yud*. We have already noted that the *hei* corresponds to the *sefirah* of understanding, which corresponds to the first *hei* of *Havayah*. The east is associated with the relatively (i.e., relative to the final *hei*) masculine *vav* of *Havayah*, leading us to associate the nun with the *vav*. Finally, the *shin*, which corresponds to the *sefirah* of kingdom (as noted) corresponds to the final *hei* of *Havayah*.

So our completed correspondence is,

face of dreidel	direction	letter of *Havayah*	*sefirah*
gimel (ג)	south	*yud* (י)	wisdom
hei (ה)	north	*hei* (ה)	understanding
nun (נ)	east	*vav* (ו)	beauty
shin (ש)	west	*hei* (ה)	kingdom

We now have a working model for understanding the essence of each of the dreidel's four faces.

Using this basic correspondence, one can even design a children's game based on spinning the dreidel. The letter on top after each spin would indicate a direction of movement on the game-board.

Rules of the Game

The most common game played with the dreidel is with nuts or almonds. Each of the players is provided with an equal quantity of nuts and play commences by placing one nut each in the pot. Each child spins the dreidel on turn. The traditional rules are that if the dreidel lands with the letter *shin* revealed the player who spun the dreidel has to add another nut to the pot (in Yiddish, the *shin* stands for *"shtel,"* meaning *"put in"*).

If the result is a *hei* (*halb*, "half," in Yiddish), the child receives half the pot (with the additional nut when there are an odd number of nuts in the pot). If the result is the *gimel* (*gantz*, meaning "all"), he wins the entire pot (and subsequently a new pot is made). And, if the result is the *nun* (*nisht*, meaning "nothing"), he does nothing and the dreidel is passed on to the next player. And so the game revolves and revolves until one of the players has won all of the nuts.

Equipped with our understanding of the dreidel's four faces we can delve deeper into the symbolism hidden in these rules.

Shin: Possessions and Ego

The *shin* requires the player to lose a nut. To understand why this is so, we need to translate the loss into the psychological realm. The *shin* as we saw corresponds to kingdom about which the *Zohar* says, "She has nothing of her own."[26] We all possess a faculty of kingdom, which is usually characterized as our ability to relate with our surroundings. When in its rectified state, our faculty of kingdom knows that all that we have been given comes from Above (in the case of *sefirot*, per se, "above" refers to the *sefirot* above kingdom). An individual with a rectified faculty of kingdom experiences a sense of lowliness in the psyche.

When kingdom is in a fallen state it is because it lacks the ability to acknowledge that all is from above, causing feelings of self-aggrandizement and self-worth to take the place of the rectified experience of lowliness. In its fallen state, kingdom becomes a breeding ground for the ego. Instead of increasing his indebtedness to the Almighty for the gifts granted him, the individual's sense of self-worth augments his possessiveness, making him feel that everything that he has is his by virtue and by right. The rectification of the psyche in such a situation is to take his possessions away, in order to impress upon him that everything he possesses is a Divine gift.

Nun: Beating Entropy

The *nun* represents a neutral state in which nothing is gained, yet nothing is lost and the game continues with the next player. The experience associated with the *nun* is that things progress naturally. Let us explain.

We explained earlier how the dreidel's Hebrew name, *sevivon*, relates to the concept of a "merchant." There are individuals who aspire to leave the world as they entered it—without having damaged anything. In a certain sense this is a negative aspiration because one should strive to be successful (spiritually and morally, of course) and not just come out unscathed. Imagine that a merchant would go to the marketplace to sell his merchandise and hope to come out with no more than enough to cover his initial investment—everybody would say he is a fool.

Every Jewish soul entered the world in order to be a merchant, i.e., to make a profit. Those who truly understand what is valuable invest their time and energy in Torah and good deeds, in their relationships with God and other people. Those that only have an external sense for the importance of making a profit spend their days chasing financial success.

Still, in the natural realm, coming out unscathed is quite an achievement because of the law of entropy, which states that everything in nature is continually losing ground to disorder.

If a natural system can end up with the same amount of energy that it started with, it is actually ahead.

When explaining the correspondence of the *nun* to the east and the *sefirah* of beauty we noted that the rising of the sun is like a herald or banner waved by God, letting us know that even nature is miraculous. The miracle of nature, as we experience it in the constantly repeating cycle of the sun (sunrise and sunset, day in and day out), is that at this level, nature does not succumb to entropy. The Creator is continually infusing nature with more energy in order to sustain its steady state. Indeed, one can thing of retaining beauty as the most illustrative example of beating entropy. Normally, as time passes, so does beauty. If any object (animate or not) can retain its beauty over time, that means it is fighting and winning the war against entropy.

Thus, when the player draws a *nun*, it is only fitting that his state remains the same: nothing gained, nothing lost, inspiring him to think about the miraculous within the natural and the need to connect with the Divine in nature in order to overcome its natural proclivity to degenerate.

Yud and Hei: A Whole and a Half

Both the *yud* and the *hei* yield a profit for the player. Since these two letters correspond to wisdom and understanding, the intellectual *sefirot*, the lesson is that when one is able to attain a state of mindfulness, there is real profit to be made. The difference is only in the amount.

Mindfulness indicates a state in which a person is wholly connected and guided by awareness of the Creator and His will as manifest through the Torah. When a person can sustain such a state, many good things come to him so that he may utilize them as part of his Divine service.

But, mindfulness can be divided into two types. The experience of mindfulness based on a feeling of self-nullification (the motivator of wisdom) before God is relatively masculine. Mindfulness based on a feeling of joy (the motivator of understanding) in serving God is relatively feminine. The coming together of masculine and feminine counterparts is described as "a whole and a half." This is one of the foundational principles for comprehending the interaction between masculine and feminine in general.

An example of the application of this principle can be seen in the difference between Shabbat and festivals. Based on verses in the Torah, the Shabbat is described as "wholly for God," while the festivals are described as "half for you and half for God."[27] This is one of the reasons for instance that it is permitted to perform actions on the festivals that are forbidden on the Shabbat, as long as they are meant to provide food for consumption ("half for you").

But, what we do gain from this idiom is that wisdom is associated with a whole and understanding with a half. Because wisdom and understanding correspond to the letters *yud* and *hei* in *Havayah*, we see that numerically they also exhibit "a whole and a half" relationship, since *yud* (י) equals 10 and *hei* (ה) equals 5.

Thus, landing on a *gimel* (the letter corresponding to wisdom) represents a state of self-nullification resulting in the player winning the whole pot. Landing on the *hei* (the letter corresponding to understanding) represents a state of joy resulting in the player winning half the pot.

Dreidel Entropy

To explain the rule that spinning a *nun* results in nothing, we used the physical concept of entropy. As it turns out we can extend this analogy further to explain the rules pertaining to all 4 letters.

We noted that the nun inspires us to look at the miraculous aspect of nature. The greatest miracle in nature is its continual recreation *ex nihilo*, something form nothing (*nisht*, beginning with the letter *nun*, as above). In fact, our ability to recognize the origin of nature's being in the Divine nothing and to then manifest this power of transforming the nothing into something is what allows us to truly and permanently overcome entropy. Translating this into the less philosophical realm of playing dreidel, to make a profit you first have to recognize nature's miraculous origin in the Divine. So, the two letters *gimel* and *hei* make the player a profit because they represent an inspired outlook on nature.

To see this, let us take a closer look at the Hebrew phrase whose initials are inscribed on the dreidel, "A great miracle occurred there" (נֵס גָּדוֹל הָיָה שָׁם). The first word in the Hebrew is "miracle" (represented by the letter *nun* on the dreidel). "Miracle" is the subject-noun of the phrase. The *gimel* stands for "great," the adjective describing the miracle, "a *great* miracle." The *hei* stands for the verb, "occurred." Like we said, first you recognize the miraculous (*nun*), then you can translate this recognition into a profit (*gimel* and *hei*). The noun, the miracle itself, is the necessary prerequisite.

The final word in the phrase, "there" falls under the realm of entropy, and so it loses energy (to the pot). This is because it implies that the miraculous has occurred somewhere else, not here. At present we are in a state of exile, a transient state of being, unable to fully utilize our connection with the Divine in order to overcome entropy as so the word "there" in its essence, falls under the law of entropy. Even changing this word to "here," in the Land of Israel, does not fully solve the problem, as the possibility of change itself implies that the word is in a transient state, dependent on location.

How to Revolutionize and Spin Reality

The Revolutionary and the Scientist

Dreidels may be said to either revolve or to spin around and around. In this section we will discuss the political revolutions and the science of spin and how they relate back to our beloved Chanukah toy.

While the verb "to revolve" in English has political significance, the verb "to spin" has scientific significance. Conceptually, the act of spinning the dreidel serves as an archetype for making things revolve around their own axis, just like a skater can revolve around his or her own axis. Players observing the unfolding game are observing the results of each particular spin, thus entering into a state of mind of spin and revolution.

Revolutions

To revolve, in the sense of revolution, is perhaps the most fundamental concept in politics: How do political revolutions start? What does it take to be a revolutionary?[28]

There are many different kinds of revolutions, with different scope. There are revolutions like the industrial or technological revolutions that affect (at least initially) only particular areas of life. There are other revolutions that simultaneously affect every aspect of our lives by changing our consciousness on all its levels filling us with new insights and understanding that spontaneously change the way we think, feel, and act. The way people feel and act can also change on a societal level. All of this has to do with revolving reality around and around itself until something wholly better and different materializes. All of this has to do with our game of dreidel.

A revolution (either industrial or political) does not necessarily require us to experience tremendous strife, or involve a great difficulty. Revolutions can also take place with pleasantness. Yet for all its placid nature, a revolution can still be total to the extent of altering the very basis of our beliefs and resulting in a political revolution (e.g., if we have a new vision and direction for the Jewish people, this does not necessarily mean that the only way to convince others is by coercion—in fact the opposite is usually true).

When we revolve (rather than spin) the dreidel on Chanukah, we are actually creating a revolution of our own, reminding ourselves of the original revolutionaries whose victory we celebrate on this holiday—the Maccabees. Commemorating the victory of the Maccabees is not merely a historical exercise, but an attempt to connect with their spirit and emulate their actions. Therefore, the type of revolution that we should have most in mind is a spiritual revolution. Focusing on this aspect of the dreidel leads us to meditate on our own innate ability to overcome foreign influence on our Jewish culture and realize our true purpose in life—to see the world with *sevivon*-like vision and bring Mashiach.

Abraham the Revolutionary

Before the Maccabee's victory and the institution of Chanukah we did not have the eight days of light to publicize the miracle to the world and one might say that we were not yet certain that we could connect with the revolutionary spirit of our forefathers. But now, through the celebration of Chanukah we can indeed be inspired in our hearts to embrace a spiritual revolution.

Earlier, we noted that every Jew is a dreidel. Now we are saying that every Jew is also a revolutionary. Abraham—the first dreidel—was also the first Jewish revolutionary. The task he took upon himself was to bring about a new covenant with God, one that would ensure that all people would be aware that the world is not separate from the Almighty. This is why the heart of every Jew—especially every Jewish child—should be implanted with a revolutionary spirit. There are many areas that a spiritual revolution has to cover and playing with the dreidel should inspire us to do so.

Scientific Meaning

In modern physics, spin is considered one of the primary properties of an elementary particle (similar to mass and charge). In many ways, a particle's spins best defines its type. The value of a particle's spin is actually a measure of its rotational symmetry. Using a graphical image, we can describe rotational symmetry as the number of times a particle will be seen in its original state if rotated 360 degrees.

Physicists identify two types of elementary particles: matter particles (e.g., the proton) also called hadrons and force-carrying particles (e.g., the photon) also called bosons. Each type carries a different value of spin. Hadrons (and their corresponding anti-matter particles) always have a half spin (or odd-integer multiple of 1/2), while bosons always have whole number spins.[29]

The five values of spin measured are:

- **1/2** (matter particles): rotating these particles 360 degrees does not return them even once to their original state. These particles need to be rotated 720 degrees to return even once to their original state.

- **1** (force-carrying particles): particles with spin 1 are most similar to the dreidel. Rotated by 360 degrees, they will return to their original state.

- **3/2** (matter particles): rotated twice around themselves, these particles will have returned to their original state 3 times.

- **2** (force-carrying particles): rotating these particles 360 degrees returns them to their original state twice.

- **0** (force-carrying particles): particles with spin 0 have perfect (i.e., an infinite amount of) rotational symmetry. Regardless of how much they are rotated they will always remain in the same original state.

Strictly speaking, if we consider the dreidel's four faces, we would define it as having spin 1, because in a 360 degree rotation, the dreidel would return to its original state once.

Still, if we consider only the top of the dreidel, which is usually round, it is easy to imagine that its spin is 0 because every point on a round circle is equivalent to any other point, in a 360 degree rotation, the top of the dreidel always remains in its original state. Building upon this interesting difference between the top of the dreidel and its four faces, we might ask whether there is a logical way to correspond the four faces to each of the non-zero values of spin.

Recall the principle noted above in the rules of playing dreidel, namely that masculine and feminine are "a whole and a half." Earlier, we applied this principle to the first two letters of *Havayah* (*yud* and *hei*) and their corresponding *sefirot*, wisdom and understanding. But, it also applies to the final two letters of *Havayah* (*vav* and *hei*), which also have a masculine to feminine relationship. Thus, we have,

letter of *Havayah*		
yud (י)	masculine	whole
hei (ה)	feminine	half
vav (ו)	masculine	whole
hei (ה)	feminine	half

The relevance to spin should be clear: whole spins are relatively masculine (i.e., bosons are masculine) and half spins are relatively feminine (i.e., hadrons are feminine).[30] Taking our cue from the photon, the force-carrying particle of electromagnetism with spin 1, and noting that in Kabbalah electromagnetism corresponds with the *vav* of *Havayah*, we can construct the following correspondence:

letter of *Havayah*	spin
tip of *yud*	0
yud (י)	2
hei (ה)	3/2
vav (ו)	1
hei (ה)	1/2

The tip of the *yud* is the fifth element of the Name *Havayah*, appearing whenever the Name *Havayah* is seen to correspond to five elements (the tip of the *yud* corresponds to the *sefirah* of crown). We can now extend our table to include the top and four faces of the dreidel, like so:

letter of *Havayah*	spin	face of dreidel
tip of *yud*	0	top
yud (י)	2	*gimel* (ג)
hei (ה)	3/2	*hei* (ה)
vav (ו)	1	*nun* (נ)
hei (ה)	1/2	*shin* (ש)

The difference between matter and force is one of the most elementary concepts both in physics and in the study of the Torah's inner dimensions—a topic that should be part of every child's (and adult's) education. What we have just seen is that playing with the dreidel can serve as a springboard to introducing modern physics and the differences between bosons and hadrons. As Maimonides writes, careful meditation on natural phenomena is necessary to promote love and fear of the Creator.

Learning How to Spin

We have seen that there are 5 spin values found in elementary particles, which he have divided into 4 primary values and an additional fifth value, spin 0. What the division of 5 into 4 and 1 alludes to is Abraham's transformation following God's commandment that he circumcise himself. Let us explain.

Up to that point, Abraham was known as Avram (אַבְרָם), whose numerical value is 243. With the commandment to circumcise himself God added a letter *hei* (ה, whose numerical value is 5) to his name, renaming him Abraham (אַבְרָהָם). The sages explain that the addition of the *hei* to his name represents the fact that with the circumcision, God gave Abraham dominion and control over five additional organs in his body, his two eyes, his two ears, and his procreative organ (where the circumcision was performed). These 5 limbs are naturally divided into 4 (eyes and ears) and 1 (the procreative organ). From that moment on, he became perfect and in consummate control over all the 248 organs of his body. Indeed, the value of his new name, Abraham (אַבְרָהָם) is 248!

So to recap, the letter *hei* and the five additional organs are the secret in Torah for the five possible spin values that modern physics finds in elementary particles.

There is a link between Abraham's change in consciousness following his circumcision and his ability to control all 248 of his limbs. With complete control of his eyes and ears, Abraham became conscious of all motion through reality occurring around him. He was therefore able to disseminate and reveal Divinity in an infinitely higher and deeper manner than previously. It follows then that the additional *hei* added to his name, which augmented his consciousness and perception gave Abraham (the first dreidel, as above) the ability to spin more freely throughout the world.

Earlier we saw that "donkey" also equals 248 (also the *gematria* of dreidel). The letters that spell "donkey" (חֲמוֹר) can also be read as "matter" (חֹמֶר). By being given dominion over all 248 limbs of his material body, Abraham became a perfect vessel for Godliness (pictured as a chariot for Godliness, by the sages). Following the circumcision, the Torah describes Abraham saddling his donkey, a metaphor, for the ability of the *tzadik*, the wholly righteous person, to master the material world and transform it into a worthy vessel for revealing God.

Mixing metaphors, Abraham became not only the master of matter (the dreidel, whose value is 248, the *gematria* of "matter"), but also a spin master of the five different spins corresponding to the spin of both matter particles and the force particles that communicate between them (*chomer*, which we have translated "matter," means "substance" in general, and includes both the "matter" particles and the "force" particles of modern physics). Incorporating the full gamut of matter and forces, Abraham now found it possible to both understand and communicate with the hearts of all different people, consciously making them aware of the one God.

As for ourselves, by spinning the dreidel, we arouse in both our hearts and the hearts of our children the revolutionary spirit needed for changing the world and making it a peaceful, productive place, worthy of serving as a dwelling place for the Almighty.

Notes:

1. Zachariah 6:12.

2. Since God creates nature anew at every moment, in effect even what we deem natural is actually an ongoing miracle, clothed in the guise of natural laws. As explained in length by the Lubavitcher Rebbe, the highest form of miracle is actually the type that can alter the course of nature while appearing to follow its laws.

3. אוֹר הַסּוֹבֵב כָּל עָלְמִין

4. אוֹר הַמְמַלֵּא כָּל עָלְמִין

5. As stressed by the Lubavitcher Rebbe, to connect with God's infinite aspect one should perform *mitzvot* from a place of infinite devotion. The more scholarly an individual is in the teachings of the Torah, the more inclined he or she is to act out of knowledge and understanding. But, dedication to the Almighty's will has to set these aside and act out of a pure aspiration to do nothing but perform His will. This is called acting out of self-sacrifice (מְסִירוּת נֶפֶשׁ) and above reason (לְמַעֲלָה מִטַּעַם וְדַעַת), the two great virtues of the Maccabees.

6. For more about the meaning of 130 and "eye," see *The Art of Education*, pp. 253ff. The discussion there also contains a deeper understanding of the connection between the dreidel and the 7-branched Menorah in the Temple. It also prompts a deeper appreciation for the dreidel's role as an educational toy.

7. *Mishnah Parah* 2:2.

8. Connecting to, following, and studying the teachings of the true leader of the generation guides us in recognizing the spiritual source and value of every group and custom within traditional Judaism.

9. As explained earlier, God's infinite nature is associated with the surrounding light and His finite nature with the inner light that

permeates reality. Chassidic teachings explain that before the first contraction, the relative brilliance (i.e., categorical superiority) of the surrounding light made it impossible to perceive God's finite nature. But, following the first contraction, His finite (immanent) nature was revealed.

10. According to Chassidic tradition it is also significant and important to calculate and contemplate the numerical value of non-Hebrew words by first transliterating them into Hebrew. The Lubavitcher Rebbe did this for various English words such as "now" (נַאוֹ).

11. Zachariah 9:9.

12. See *Ta'anit* 16a.

13. Another word for play, טַל (as in the name Talia), is also etymologically related to the two letters טַ.

14. See *Berachot* 48a.

15. Extending the analogy, we may say that Abraham riding his donkey is tantamount to his spinning all of materiality ("donkey" equals "matter," as we will see) in an effort to uplift it to Divine consciousness.

16. Regarding the wondrous nature of the return to God, see "Converting the Wisdom of the Nations" on our website (www.inner.org). Also see an expanded version of this article in our upcoming volume *Integrating Torah and Science*.

17. Psalms 72:17. See *The Hebrew Letters*, p. 208.

18. Joshua 14:15.

19. Genesis 12:1.

20. Ibid. 12:9 and *Rashi* there. See also *Torat Menachem 5713* Volume 1, p. 248.

21. See *Torah Or* 34d, *Likutei Torah Bamidbar* 32d, etc.

22. *Rambam, Hilchot Temidin Umusafin* 3:16.

The idea that gold is composed of the numbers 5 and 2 describes its origin and purpose. 5 alludes to its origin. Gold's spiritual origin is the *sefirah* of understanding, which corresponds to the first *hei* of *Havayah*, whose value is 5. 2 alludes gold's ultimate purpose. The sages teach (Bereishit Rabbah 16:2) that God created gold for use solely in His house, the Holy Temple. The word "house" (בַּיִת, as in בֵּית הַמִּקְדָּשׁ) is the name of the letter *bet* (ב) whose value is 2.

23. Job 37:22.

24. We noted earlier that some dreidels have the letter *pei* (פ) instead of a *shin* and the reason for this. As a word, the letter *pei* means "mouth" (פֶּה) the part of the body corresponding to the *sefirah* of kingdom and to the Divine Presence (see Introduction to *Tikunei Zohar*).

25. *Bava Batra* 25b.

26. *Zohar* II, 215a.

27. *Pesachim* 68b.

28. Spin has also taken on a political meaning in the past few decades and is used to denote control of the relationship between politics and the media.

29. The spin value of matter particles is always a fraction. The word "fraction," in both English and Hebrew (שֶׁבֶר), is synonymous with breaking and alludes to the breaking of the vessels, the origin of our current perception of matter according to Kabbalah.

30. The conceptual corollary of this statement is indeed true: force (bosons) is masculine relative to matter (hadrons).